Shakespeare

& Love Sonnets

First published in Great Britain by Brockhampton Press,
20 Bloomsbury Street, London WC1B 3QA.

Copyright © 1996 Brockhampton Press

This 1999 edition is published by Gramercy Books™, an imprint of
Random House Value Publishing, Inc., 201 East 50th Street, New York, N.Y. 10022.
Reprint 2000
Gramercy Books™ and colophon are trademarks of
Random House Value Publishing, Inc.

Random House
New York • Toronto • London • Sydney • Auckland
http://www.randomhouse.com/

Created and produced by Flame Tree Publishing,
part of The Foundry Creative Media Company Limited,
Crabtree Hall, Crabtree Lane, Fulham, London SW6 6TY.

Special thanks to
Kate Brown and Kelley Doak for their work on this series.

Printed and bound in U. A. E.

A CIP catalog record for this book is available from the Library of Congress.

ISBN 0-517-16107-9

8 7 6 5 4 3 2 1

Shakespeare
& Love Sonnets

Selected and written by
O. B. Duane

Gramercy Books
New York

Contents

Introduction

LTHOUGH POPULARLY conceived as a Shakespearean invention, the sonnet form actually dates back to the late thirteenth century when the Italian poet Alighieri Dante first wrote verses of a similar length and rhythmic scheme. But it was Francesco Petrarch, Dante's successor, who emerged as the most significant of the earliest sonneteers, having a profound and pervasive influence on the majority of later Elizabethan lyrical poets.

The sonnet, whose name is derived from the Italian word meaning 'a little sound', was first introduced into England by Sir Thomas Wyatt in the early sixteenth century. Wyatt, who was born and raised in Kent and later educated at Cambridge, began writing sonnets closely mimicking the Italian structure and style shortly after a visit to that country in 1527. The majority of Wyatt's sonnets and those of his imitators, including the Earl of Surrey, appeared in Richard Tottel's *Miscellany of Songs and Sonnets*, published in 1557, the year before Elizabeth I ascended the throne. During the first decade of her reign, very few sonnets seemed to have been produced, but with the writing of Sir Philip Sidney's sequence *Astrophel and Stella* in 1582, Samuel Daniel's *Delia* verses in 1592, and Sir Edmund Spenser's *Amoretti* series, printed in 1595, the sonnet was re-born as the most popular form of Elizabethan lyric.

Although none of Sir Philip Sidney's work was ever published during his lifetime, a great deal of it was circulated in manuscript form, promoting his influence as one of the most important progressors of the sonnet since the early Tudor poets. He was a very popular man at court and was also much admired by his contemporaries as a great statesman, scholar and literary talent. From 1568-71, Sidney

was educated at Christ Church, Oxford, after which time he journeyed to Italy where he steeped himself in the nation's art, literature and music. The 108 sonnets which form the *Astrophel and Stella* sequence were dedicated to Penelope Devereux, daughter of the Earl of Essex, and trace the unrequited love of Astrophel, meaning 'lover of a star', for Stella, his 'star'. Many consider these verses to be Sidney's best work and few would argue that they fostered the passion for love sonnets which dominated the 1590s. Sidney's other notable works included his pastoral romance *Arcadia* and his *Apologie for Poetrie*. He died an heroic death at the relatively young age of thirty-two, having sustained a musket wound from which he never properly recovered, at the battle of Zutphen in the Netherlands.

During the winter of 1578-9, Sidney had met up with Sir Edmund Spenser at the home of Sidney's uncle, the Earl of Leicester, who at that time also acted as Spenser's patron. The son of a London merchant, Spenser was educated at Cambridge and made his literary debut with his collection of twelve pastoral poems entitled *The Shepherds' Calendar*, published in 1579 and dedicated to Sidney. He spent the majority of his crucially formative years, from 1580 to 1598, in Ireland acting as secretary to Lord Grey of Wilton, Deputy of Ireland. It was here that he worked on his most famous work, *The Faerie Queene*, an allegorical poem of epic proportions, written in honour of Elizabeth I and published in six books between 1598 and 1596. Spenser's *Amoretti* sonnets – eighty-eight of them in total – were inspired by his wooing of Elizabeth Boyle, whom he married in 1594.

The gifted writer and intellectual genius, Sir Walter Raleigh, whom Queen Elizabeth once acknowledged as her favourite courtier, is probably best remembered for his numerous prose works, particularly his ambitious book, *The History of the World*, which he worked on during his long

LIP SIDNEY.

who giues him selfe, may well his picture
els weare it vayne since both short tyme d

imprisonment in the Tower of London under Elizabeth's successor, James I. It was Raleigh, however, who encouraged Spenser in his major work, *The Fairie Queene*, when he visited him in Ireland in 1580, and it was also Raleigh who, as a highly accomplished poet in his own right, wrote the prefatory sonnet to Spenser's great narrative poem. Raleigh fell out of favour with the Queen when she discovered he had secretly married one of her Maids of Honour, Elizabeth Throckmorton. He fared much worse under James I, however, and in October 1916 faced a number of spurious charges of treason for which he was tried and subsequently executed.

Not least among the contemporary poets Shakespeare would have turned to for early instruction in the art of sonnet-writing was Samuel Daniel, popular as a court poet in his day. Daniel, who was educated at Oxford, became a member of the household of the Countess of Pembroke, Sir Philip Sidney's sister, during the 1590s. Thus he was heavily influenced by Sidney's sequence of sonnets exploring his love for Penelope Devereux. Daniel's *Delia* sonnets were dedicated to the Countess and were published in 1592, the year Shakespeare is thought to have penned the first of his own verses.

The Elizabethan period of lyrical love poetry is primarily regarded as the golden age of Shakespeare's sonnet-writing, with few of his contemporaries gaining recognition as legitimate sonneteers. It is true, of course, to say that Shakespeare's sonnets are some of the most inspired and highly polished of the era, but they none the less owe a great deal to the work of his predecessors who helped to establish the framework and traditions of the form to which Shakespeare added his own unique depth of passion and artistic genius.

William Shakespeare was born in Stratford-upon-Avon in 1564, the son of a glover, merchant and relatively prominent figure who acted as a local justice of the peace. Only a limited amount is known about Shakespeare's youth, although it is certain that he attended an Elizabethan grammar school in Stratford, an establishment with high standards of education where children were taught mostly through Latin. He seems also to have been a fairly wild though innocent young man, and in 1582, when he was eighteen years old, he married Anne Hathaway, a woman eight years his senior who had fallen pregnant by him. Little or no information on his beginnings as a writer, or on his early theatrical career, has ever come to light. Within a few years of his marriage, however, it is believed that Shakespeare came to London, using the capital as his professional base, and working hard there to build his career as an actor and writer. He probably began to write for the stage in the late 1580s and had certainly established a sound reputation for himself as a dramatist by 1592.

Shakespeare's sonnets, which many consider to be some of the finest poems in the English language, are thought to have been written between 1592 and 1594/5. There are 154 sonnets in the complete sequence and although they were not published until 1609, they were already in circulation among Shakespeare's private friends by 1598. Sonnets 1-126 follow a distinct narrative thread centring on a theme of the poet's love and affection for a beautiful youth, whose identity has now been almost universally acknowledged as that of Shakespeare's patron, Henry Wriothesley, third Earl of Southampton. The first seventeen sonnets focus on a time-honoured Elizabethan theme of beauty's subservience to the ravages of time, and in these verses Shakespeare urges the young man to marry so that his beauty may live on through his offspring. The sequence of 108 sonnets which follow, echoing Sidney's numerical structure, explore the greater complexities of the relationship between the poet and his patron. These monumental verses, in which the density and intimacy of emotion is at times quite overwhelming, exhibit a striking range of imagery, metaphor, tone and rhythm.

Sonnets 127-152 take up a new theme of Shakespeare's affair with Emalia Lanier, the young, dark beauty he was entirely infatuated by and who eventually became his mistress. This group of sonnets also covers the Earl of Southampton's involvement with the same woman, becoming more emotionally charged as feelings of betrayal and inefficacy rise to the surface, demanding poetic expression.

During the final decade of the sixteenth century, almost all sonnets which appeared were in Shakespearean form using the rhyming scheme: ab ab cd cd ef ef gg. But with the emergence of the Metaphysical poets, of whom John Donne is considered the first example, greater experimentation with the sonnet form occurred. Donne's *Divine Meditations*, it has to be said, revert to a more obviously traditional form, but his early love sonnets comply with the word's broader meaning. His love poems did not follow any specific Petrarchan rhythmic design, but were 'little songs', and therefore legitimate sonnets in the general sense, adopting a more varied lyric approach and refusing to follow in any particular narrative sequence. The verses of John Donne reproduced here share many of the themes of other Elizabethan love poets and are taken from *Songs and Sonnets*, a collection which remained unpublished until 1633, but which is thought to have been written shortly after the turn of the century.

Two sonnets of John Milton, the youngest of all the group, conclude this volume. Their overall structure, thematic content, and rhythmic pattern are a reversion to the Petrarchan tradition, which surely serves as a powerful indication of the ongoing popularity of the sonnet form and of every great poet's desire, from Sidney, through to Keats and Browning, to master its usage and perfect its design.

Author's Note

This book opens with a comprehensive selection of the most popular sonnets of Shakespeare, reproduced from *The Alexander Text of the Complete Works of Shakespeare*. The works of other sonneteers follow in chronological order of the poets' date of birth.

William Shakespeare

II

When forty winters shall besiege thy brow,
And dig deep trenches in thy beauty's field,
Thy youth's proud livery, so gaz'd on now,
Will be a tatter'd weed of small worth held.
Then, being ask'd where all thy beauty lies,
Where all the treasure of thy lusty days,
To say within thine own deep-sunken eyes
Were an all-eating shame and thriftless praise.
How much more praise deserv'd thy beauty's use,
If thou couldst answer 'This fair child of mine
Shall sum my count, and make my old excuse',
Proving his beauty by succession thine!
This were to be new made when thou art old,
And see thy blood warm when thou feel'st it cold.

III

Look in thy glass, and tell the face thou viewest
Now is the time that face should form another;
Whose fresh repair if now thou not renewest,
Thou dost beguile the world, unbless some mother.
For where is she so fair whose unear'd womb
Disdains the tillage of thy husbandry?
Or who is he so fond will be the tomb
Of his self-love, to stop posterity?
Thou art thy mother's glass, and she in thee
Calls back the lovely April of her prime;
So thou through windows of thine age shalt see,
Despite of wrinkles, this thy golden time.
But if thou live rememb'red not to be,
Die single, and thine image dies with thee.

XI

As fast as thou shalt wane, so fast thou grow'st
In one of thine, from that which thou departest;
And that fresh blood which youngly thou bestow'st
Thou may'st call thine when thou from youth convertest.
Herein lives wisdom, beauty, and increase;
Without this folly, age, and cold decay.
If all were minded so, the times should cease,
And threescore year would make the world away.
Let those whom Nature hath not made for store,
Harsh, featureless and rude, barrenly perish.
Look whom she best endow'd she gave the more;
Which bounteous gift thou shouldst in bounty cherish;
She carv'd thee for her seal, and meant thereby
Thou shouldst print more, not let that copy die.

XV

When I consider every thing that grows
Holds in perfection but a little moment,
That this huge stage presenteth nought but shows
Whereon the stars in secret influence comment;
When I perceive that men as plants increase,
Cheered and check'd even by the self-same sky,
Vaunt in their youthful sap, at height decrease,
And wear their brave state out of memory;
Then the conceit of this inconstant stay
Sets you most rich in youth before my sight,
Where wasteful Time debateth with Decay
To change your day of youth to sullied night;
And, all in war with Time for love of you,
As he takes from you, I engraft you new.

XVII

Who will believe my verse in time to come,
If it were fill'd with your most high deserts?
Though yet, heaven knows, it is but as a tomb
Which hides your life and shows not half your parts.
If I could write the beauty of your eyes
And in fresh numbers number all your graces,
The age to come would say 'This poet lies;

Such heavenly touches ne'er touch'd earthly faces'.
So should my papers, yellowed with their age,
Be scorn'd, like old men of less truth than tongue;
And your true rights be term'd a poet's rage,
And stretched metre of an antique song.
But were some child of yours alive that time,
You should live twice – in it, and in my rhyme.

XVIII

Shall I compare thee to a summer's day?
Thou art more lovely and more temperate.
Rough winds do shake the darling buds of May,
And summer's lease hath all too short a date:
Sometime too hot the eye of heaven shines,
And often is his gold complexion dimm'd;
And every fair from fair some time declines,

By chance, or nature's changing course untrimm'd;
But thy eternal summer shall not fade
Nor lose possession of that fair thou ow'st;
Nor shall Death brag thou wand'rest in his shade,
When in eternal lines to time thou grow'st.
So long as men can breathe or eyes can see,
So long lives this, and this gives life to thee.

XIX

Devouring Time, blunt thou the lion's paws,
And make the earth devour her own sweet brood;
Pluck the keen teeth from the fierce tiger's jaws,
And burn the long-liv'd phoenix in her blood;
Make glad and sorry seasons as thou fleet'st,
And do whate'er thou wilt, swift-footed Time,
To the wide world and all her fading sweets;
But I forbid thee one most heinous crime:
O, carve not with thy hours my love's fair brow,
Nor draw no lines there with thine antique pen;
Him in thy course untainted do allow
For beauty's pattern to succeeding men.
Yet, do thy worst, old Time. Despite thy wrong,
My love shall in my verse ever live young.

XXIII

As an unperfect actor on the stage
Who with his fear is put besides his part,
Or some fierce thing replete with too much rage,
Whose strength's abundance weakens his own heart;
So I, for fear of trust, forget to say
The perfect ceremony of love's rite,
And in mine own love's strength seem to decay,
O'ercharg'd with burthen of mine own love's might.
O, let my looks be then the eloquence
And dumb presagers of my speaking breast;
Who plead for love, and look for recompense,
More than that tongue that more hath more express'd.
O, learn to read what silent love hath writ!
To hear with eyes belongs to love's fine wit.

XXVII

Weary with toil, I haste me to my bed,
The dear repose for limbs with travel tired;
But then begins a journey in my head
To work my mind, when body's work's expired;
For then my thoughts, from far where I abide,
Intend a zealous pilgrimage to thee,
And keep my drooping eyelids open wide,
Looking on darkness which the blind do see;
Save that my soul's imaginary sight
Presents thy shadow to my sightless view,
Which, like a jewel hung in ghastly night,
Makes black night beauteous and her old face new.
Lo, thus, by day my limbs, by night my mind,
For thee, and for myself, no quiet find.

XXX

When to the sessions of sweet silent thought
I summon up remembrance of things past,
I sigh the lack of many a thing I sought,
And with old woes new wail my dear time's waste.
Then can I drown an eye, unus'd to flow,
For precious friends hid in death's dateless night,
And weep afresh love's long since cancell'd woe,
And moan th' expense of many a vanish'd sight.
Then can I grieve at grievances foregone,
And heavily from woe to woe tell o'er
The sad account of fore-bemoaned moan,
Which I new pay as if not paid before.
But if the while I think on thee, dear friend,
All losses are restor'd and sorrows end.

XXXIV

Why didst thou promise such a beauteous day,
And make me travel forth without my cloak,
To let base clouds o'ertake me in my way,
Hiding thy brav'ry in their rotten smoke?
'Tis not enough that through the cloud thou break
To dry the rain on my storm-beaten face,
For no man well of such a salve can speak
That heals the wound and cures not the disgrace.
Nor can thy shame give physic to my grief;
Though thou repent, yet I have still the loss.
Th' offender's sorrow lends but weak relief
To him that bears the strong offence's cross.
Ah! but those tears are pearls which thy love sheds,
And they are rich, and ransom all ill deeds.

XXXV

No more be griev'd at that which thou hast done:
Roses have thorns, and silver fountains mud;
Clouds and eclipses stain both moon and sun,
And loathsome canker lives in sweetest bud.
All men make faults, and even I in this,
Authorizing thy trespass with compare,
Myself corrupting, salving thy amiss,
Excusing thy sins more than thy sins are;
For to thy sensual fault I bring in sense –
Thy adverse party is thy advocate –
And 'gainst myself a lawful plea commence;
Such civil war is in my love and hate
That I an accessary needs must be
To that sweet thief which sourly robs from me.

XXXVI

Let me confess that we two must be twain,
Although our undivided loves are one;
So shall those blots that do with me remain,
Without thy help, by me be borne alone.
In our two loves there is but one respect,
Though in our lives a separable spite,
Which though it alters not love's sole effect,
Yet doth it steal sweet hours from love's delight.
I may not evermore acknowledge thee,
Lest my bewailèd guilt should do thee shame;
Nor thou with public kindness honour me,
Unless thou take that honour from thy name.
But do not so; I love thee in such sort
As, thou being mine, mine is thy good report.

XL

Take all my loves, my love, yea, take them all;
What hast thou then more than thou hadst before?
No love, my love, that thou mayst true love call;
All mine was thine before thou hadst this more.
Then if for my love thou my love receivest,
I cannot blame thee, for my love thou usest;
But yet be blam'd, if thou thyself deceivest
By wilful taste of what thyself refusest.
I do forgive thy robb'ry, gentle thief,
Although thou steal thee all my poverty;
And yet love knows it is a greater grief
To bear love's wrong than hate's known injury.
Lascivious grace, in whom all ill well shows,
Kill me with spites; yet we must not be foes.

XLVII

Betwixt mine eye and heart a league is took,
And each doth good turns now unto the other.
When that mine eye is famish'd for a look,
Or heart in love with sighs himself doth smother;
With my love's picture then my eye doth feast,
And to the painted banquet bids my heart;
Another time mine eye is my heart's guest,
And in his thoughts of love doth share a part;
So, either by thy picture or my love,
Thyself away art present still with me;
For thou not farther than my thoughts canst move,
And I am still with them and they with thee;
Or if they sleep, thy picture in my sight
Awakes my heart to heart's and eye's delight.

XLVIII

How careful was I when I took my way,
Each trifle under truest bars to thrust,
That to my use it might unused stay
From hands of falsehood, in sure wards of trust!
But thou, to whom my jewels trifles are,
Most worthy comfort, now my greatest grief,
Thou, best of dearest, and mine only care,
Art left the prey of every vulgar thief.
Thee have I not lock'd up in any chest,
Save where thou art not, though I feel thou art,
Within the gentle closure of my breast,
From whence at pleasure thou mayst come and part;
And even thence thou wilt be stol'n, I fear,
For truth proves thievish for a prize so dear.

LV

Not marble nor the gilded monuments
Of princes shall outlive this pow'rful rhyme;
But you shall shine more bright in these contents
Than unswept stone, besmear'd with sluttish time.
When wasteful war shall statues overturn,
And broils root out the work of masonry,
Nor Mars his sword nor war's quick fire shall burn
The living record of your memory.
'Gainst death and all-oblivious enmity
Shall you pace forth; your praise shall still find room,
Even in the eyes of all posterity
That wear this world out to the ending doom.
So, till the judgment that yourself arise,
You live in this, and dwell in lover's eyes.

LX

Like as the waves make towards the pebbled shore,
So do our minutes hasten to their end;
Each changing place with that which goes before,
In sequent toil all forwards do contend.
Nativity, once in the main of light,
Crawls to maturity, wherewith being crown'd,
Crooked eclipses 'gainst his glory fight,
And Time that gave doth now his gift confound.
Time doth transfix the flourish set on youth,
And delves the parallels in beauty's brow,
Feeds on the rarities of nature's truth,
And nothing stands but for his scythe to mow.
And yet to times in hope my verse shall stand,
Praising thy worth, despite his cruel hand.

LXXIII

That time of year thou mayst in me behold
When yellow leaves, or none, or few, do hang
Upon those boughs which shake against the cold,
Bare ruin'd choirs where late the sweet birds sang.
In me thou see'st the twilight of such day
As after sunset fadeth in the west,
Which by and by black night doth take away,
Death's second self, that seals up all in rest.
In me thou seest the glowing of such fire
That on the ashes of his youth doth lie,
As the death-bed whereon it must expire,
Consum'd with that which it was nourish'd by.
This thou perceiv'st, which makes thy love more strong,
To love that well which thou must leave ere long.

CIV

To me, fair friend, you never can be old,
For as you were when first your eye I ey'd,
Such seems your beauty still. Three winters cold
Have from the forests shook three summers' pride,
Three beauteous springs to yellow autumn turn'd
In process of the seasons have I seen,
Three April perfumes in three hot Junes burn'd,
Since first I saw you fresh, which yet are green.
Ah, yet doth beauty, like a dial-hand,
Steal from his figure, and no pace perceiv'd;
So your sweet hue, which methinks still doth stand,
Hath motion, and mine eye may be deceiv'd.
For fear of which, hear this, thou age unbred:
Ere you were born was beauty's summer dead.

CIX

O, never say that I was false of heart,
Though absence seem'd my flame to qualify!
As easy might I from my self depart
As from my soul, which in thy breast doth lie:
That is my home of love. If I have rang'd,
Like him that travels, I return again,
Just to the time, not with the time exchang'd,
So that my self bring water for my stain.
Never believe, though in my nature reign'd
All frailties that besiege all kinds of blood,
That it could so preposterously be stain'd
To leave for nothing all thy sum of good;
For nothing this wide universe I call
Save thou, my rose; in it thou art my all.

CXVI

Let me not to the marriage of true minds
Admit impediments. Love is not love
Which alters when it alteration finds,
Or bends with the remover to remove.
O, no! it is an ever-fixed mark,
That looks on tempests and is never shaken;
It is the star to every wand'ring bark,
Whose worth's unknown, although his height be taken.
Love's not Time's fool, though rosy lips and cheeks
Within his bending sickle's compass come;
Love alters not with his brief hours and weeks,
But bears it out even to the edge of doom.
If this be error, and upon me prov'd,
I never writ, nor no man ever lov'd.

CXXX

My mistress' eyes are nothing like the sun;
  Coral is far more red than her lips' red;
If snow be white, why then her breasts are dun;
If hairs be wires, black wires grow on her head.
I have seen roses damask'd, red and white,
  But no such roses see I in her cheeks;
And in some perfumes is there more delight
Than in the breath that from my mistress reeks.
I love to hear her speak, yet well I know
That music hath a far more pleasing sound;
  I grant I never saw a goddess go –
My mistress, when she walks, treads on the ground.
And yet, by heaven, I think my love as rare
  As any she belied with false compare.

CXLV

Those lips that Love's own hand did make
Breath'd forth the sound that said 'I hate'
To me that languish'd for her sake;
But when she saw my woeful state,
Straight in her heart did mercy come,
Chiding that tongue that ever sweet
Was us'd in giving gentle doom;
And taught it thus anew to greet:
'I hate' she alter'd with an end
That follow'd it as gentle day
Doth follow night, who like a fiend
From heaven to hell is flown away:
'I hate' from hate away she threw,
And sav'd my life, saying 'not you'.

CXLVII

My love is as a fever, longing still
For that which longer nurseth the disease;
Feeding on that which doth preserve the ill,
Th' uncertain sickly appetite to please.
My Reason, the physician to my Love,
Angry that his prescriptions are not kept,
Hath left me, and I desperate now approve
Desire is death, which physic did except.
Past cure I am, now reason is past care,
And frantic mad with evermore unrest;
My thoughts and my discourse as madmen's are,
At random from the truth vainly express'd;
For I have sworn thee fair, and thought thee bright,
Who art as black as hell, as dark as night.

Sir Thomas Wyatt

X

The long love that in my thought doth harbour
And in mine heart doth keep his residence
Into my face presseth with bold pretence
And therein campeth, spreading his banner.
She that me learneth to love and suffer
And will that my trust and lust's negligence
Be reined by reason, shame, and reverence,
With his hardiness taketh displeasure.
Wherewithal unto the heart's forest he fleeth,
Leaving his enterprise with pain and cry,
And there him hideth and not appeareth.
What may I do when my master feareth,
But in the field with him to live and die?
For good is the life ending faithfully.

XIV

My heart I gave thee, not to do it pain;
But to preserve, it was to thee taken.
I served thee, not to be forsaken,
But that I should be rewarded again.
I was content thy servant to remain
But not to be paid under this fashion.
Now since in thee is none other reason,
Displease thee not if that I do refrain,
Unsatiate of my woe and thy desire,
Assured by craft to excuse thy fault.
But since it please thee to feign a default,
Farewell, I say, parting from the fire:
For he that believeth bearing in hand,
Plougheth in water and soweth in the sand.

XXV

The lively sparks that issue from those eyes
Against the which ne vaileth no defence
Have pressed mine heart and done it none offence
With quaking pleasure more than once or twice.
Was never man could anything devise
The sunbeams to turn with so great vehemence
To daze man's sight, as by their bright presence
Dazed am I, much like unto the guise
Of one ystricken with dint of lightning,
Blinded with the stroke, erring here and there.
So call I for help, I not when ne where,
The pain of my fall patiently bearing.
For after the blaze, as is no wonder,
Of deadly 'Nay' hear I the fearful thunder.

XXXI

Farewell, Love, and all thy laws forever.
Thy baited hooks shall tangle me no more.
Senec and Plato call me from thy lore
To perfect wealth my wit for to endeavour.
In blind error when I did persevere,
Thy sharp repulse that pricketh ay so sore
Hath taught me to set in trifles no store
And scape forth since liberty is lever.
Therefore farewell. Go trouble younger hearts
And in me claim no more authority.
With idle youth go use thy property
And thereon spend thy many brittle darts:
For hitherto though I have lost all my time,
Me lusteth no longer rotten boughs to climb.

Edmund Spenser

TO THE RIGHT NOBLE AND VALOROUS KNIGHT,
SIR WALTER RALEIGH

To thee, that art the sommers Nightingale,
Thy sovereign Goddesses most dear delight,
Why do I send this rustic madrigal,
That may thy tuneful ear unseason quite?
Thou only fit this argument to write,
In whose high thoughts pleasure hath built her bower,
And dainty love learn'd sweetly to indite.
My rhymes I know unsavoury and sour,
To taste the streams that, like a golden shower,
Flow from thy fruitful head, of thy love's praise;
Fitter, perhaps, to thunder martial stour,
When so thee list thy lofty muse to raise:
Yet, till that thou thy poem wilt make known,
Let thy fair Cinthias praises be thus rudely shown.

TO THE RIGHT HONOURABLE AND MOST VERTUOUS LADY
THE COUNTESSE OF PENBROKE

Remembrance of that most heroic spirit,
The heaven's pride, the glory of our days,
Which now triumpheth, through immortal merit
Of his brave virtues, crown'd with lasting bays
Of heavenly bliss and everlasting praise;
Who first my muse did lift out of the floor,
To sing his sweet delights in lowly lays;
Bids me, most noble Lady, to adore
His goodly image, living evermore
In the divine resemblance of your face;
Which with your virtues ye embellish more,
And native beauty deck with heavenly grace:
For his, and for your own especial sake,
Vouchsafe from him this token in good worth to take.

TO THE MOST VIRTUOUS AND BEAUTIFUL LADY,
THE LADY CAREW

Ne may I, without blot of endless blame,
You, fairest Lady, leave out of this place;
But with remembrance of your gracious name,
Wherewith that courtly garland most ye grace
And deck the world, adorn these verses base.
Not that these few lines can in them comprise
Those glorious ornaments of heavenly grace,
Wherewith ye triumph over feeble eyes,
And in subdued hearts do tyrannise;
For thereunto doth need a golden quill,
And silver leaves, them rightly to devise;
But to make humble present of good will:
Which, whenas timely means it purchase may,
In ampler wise it self will forth display.

From *AMORETTI*

XXXIV

Like as a ship that through the ocean wide
By conduct of some star doth make her way,
Whenas a storm hath dimmed her trusty guide,
Out of her course doth wander far astray,
So I whose star, that wont with her bright ray
Me to direct, with clouds is overcast,
Do wander now in darkness and dismay,
Through hidden perils round about me placed.
Yet hope I well that, when this storm is past,
My Helice, the lodestar of my life,
Will shine again, and look on me at last,
With lovely light to clear my cloudy grief.
Till then I wander careful, comfortless,
In secret sorrow and sad pensiveness.

LXI

The glorious image of the Maker's beauty,
My sovereign saint, the idol of my thought,
Dare not henceforth above the bounds of duty
T' accuse of pride, or rashly blame for aught.
For, being as she is divinely wrought,
And of the brood of angels heavenly born,
And with the crew of blessed saints upbrought,

Each of which did her with their gifts adorn,
The bud of joy, the blossom of the morn,
The beam of light, whom mortal eyes admire,
What reason is it then but she should scorn
Base things, that too her love too bold aspire?
Such heavenly forms ought rather worshipped be,
Than dare be loved by men of mean degree.

LXXV

One day I wrote her name upon the strand,
But came the waves and washed it away;
Again I wrote it with a second hand,
But came the tide and made my pains his prey.
'Vain man', said she, 'that doest in vain essay
A mortal thing so to immortalise,
For I myself shall like to this decay,
And eke my name be wiped out likewise'.
'Not so', quod I, 'let baser things devise
To die in dust, but you shall live by fame;
My verse your virtues rare shall eternise,
And in the heavens write your glorious name.
Where, whenas death shall all the world subdue,
Our love shall live, and later life renew.'

Sir Walter Raleigh

THE PHOENIX NEST
From *LIKE TO A HERMIT*

Like to a hermit poor in place obscure,
I mean to spend my days of endless doubt,
To wail such woes as time cannot recure,
Where none but Love shall ever find me out.
My food shall be of care and sorrow made,
My drink nought else but tears fallen from mine eyes,
And for my light, in such obscured shade,
The flames shall serve, which from my heart arise.
A gown of gray my body shall attire,
My staff of broken hope whereon I'll stay;
Of late repentance, linked with long desire,
The couch is framed wheron my limbs I'll lay.
And at my gate despair shall linger still,
To let in death when Love and Fortune will.

WIT'S INTERPRETER
From OUR PASSIONS ARE MOST LIKE

Our passions are most like to floods and streams;
The shallow murmur, but the deep are dumb.
So, when affections yield discourse, it seems
The bottom is but shallow whence they come.
They that are rich in words must needs discover
That they are poor in that which makes a lover.

COMMENDATORY VERSE PUBLISHED WITH
SPENSER'S FAERIE QUEENE

Methought I saw the grave, where Laura lay,
Within that temple, where the vestal flame
Was wont to burn, and, passing by that way,
To see that buried dust of living fame,
Whose tomb fair Love and fairer Virtue kept,
All suddenly I saw the Fairy Queen;
At whose approach the soul of Petrarch wept,
And from thenceforth those graces were not seen,
For they this Queen attended, in whose stead
Oblivion laid him down on Laura's hearse.
Hereat the hardest stones were seen to bleed,
And groans of buried ghosts the heavens did pierce.
Where Homer's spright did tremble all for grief,
And cursed th'access of that celestial thief.

Sir Philip Sidney

From *ASTROPHEL AND STELLA*

I

Loving in truth, and fain in verse my love to show,
That she, dear She, might take some pleasure of my pain,
Pleasure might cause her read, reading might make her know,
Knowledge might pity win, and pity grace obtain,
I sought fit words to paint the blackest face of woe;
Studying inventions fine, her wits to entertain,
Oft turning others' leaves, to see if thence would flow
Some fresh and fruitful showers upon my sun-burn'd brain.
But words came halting forth, wanting Invention's stay;
Invention, Nature's child, fled step-dame Study's blows;
And others' feet still seem'd but strangers in my way.
Thus, great with child to speak, and helpless in my throes,
Biting my truant pen, beating myself for spite,
'Fool,' said my Muse to me, 'look in thy heart and write.'

VI

Some lovers speak, when they their Muses entertain,
Of hopes begot by fear, of wot not what desires,
Of force of heavenly beams infusing hellish pain,
Of living deaths, dear wounds, fair storms, and freezing fires:
Someone his song in Jove and Jove's strange tales attires,
'Broidered with bulls and swans, powdered with golden rain:
Another humbler wit to shepherd's pipe retires,
Yet hiding royal blood full oft in rural vein.
To some a sweetest plaint a sweetest style affords:
While tears pour out his ink, and sighs
breathe out his words,
His paper pale despair, and pain his pen doth move.
I can speak what I feel, and feel as much as they,
But think that all the map of my state I display
When trembling voice brings forth that I do Stella love.

XIV

Alas, have I not pain enough, my friend,
Upon whose breast a fiercer gripe doth tire
Than did on him who first stole down the fire,
While Love on me doth all his quiver spend—
But with your rhubarb words ye must contend,
To grieve me worse, in saying that Desire
Doth plunge my well-form'd soul even in the mire
Of sinful thoughts, which do in ruin end.
If that be sin which doth the manners frame,
Well staid with truth in word and faith of deed,
Ready of wit, and fearing nought but shame;
If that be sin, which in fix'd hearts doth breed
A loathing of all loose unchastity,
Then love is sin, and let me sinful be.

XXVIII

You that with allegory's curious frame
Of others' children changelings use to make,
With me those pains, for God's sake, do not take;
I list not dig so deep for brazen fame.
When I say Stella, I do mean the same
Princess of beauty, for whose only sake
The reins of Love I love, though never slack,
And joy therein, though nations count it shame.
I beg no subject to use eloquence,
Nor in hid ways do guide philosophy;
Look at my hands for no such quintessence;
But know that I in pure simplicity
Breathe out the flames which burn within my heart,
Love only reading unto me this art.

XXXI

With how sad steps, O Moon, thou climb'st the skies,
How silently, and with how wan a face.
What, may it be that even in heavenly place
That busy archer his sharp arrows tries?
Sure, if that long-with-love-acquainted eyes
Can judge of love, thou feel'st a lover's case;
I read it in thy looks; thy languisht grace,
To me that feel the like, thy state descries.
Then even of fellowship, O Moon, tell me,
Is constant love deemed there but want of wit?
Are beauties there as proud as here they be?
Do they above love to be loved, and yet
Those lovers scorn whom that love doth posess?
Do they call virtue there ungratefulness?

LXXIV

I never drank of Aganippe well,
Nor ever did in shade of Tempe sit,
And Muses scorn with vulgar brains to dwell,
Poor layman I, for sacred rites unfit.
Some do I hear of poets' fury tell,
But (God wot) wot not what they mean by it;
And this I swear by blackest brook of hell,
I am no pick-purse of another's wit.
How falls it then, that with so smooth an ease
My thoughts I speak, and what I speak doth flow
In verse, and that my verse best wits doth please?
Guess we the cause. 'What, is it thus?' Fie, no.
'Or so?' Much less. 'How then?' Sure thus it is:
My lips are sweet, inspired with Stella's kiss.

LXXXII

Nymph of the garden where all beauties be,
Beauties which do in excellency pass
His who till death look'd in a wat'ry glass,
Or hers whom nak'd the Trojan boy did see;
Sweet garden-nymph, which keeps the cherry-tree
Whose fruit doth far th' Esperian taste surpass,
Most sweet-fair, most fair-sweet, do not, alas,
From coming near those cherries banish me.
For though, full of desire, empty of wit,
Admitted late by your best-gracèd grace,
I caught at one of them, a hungry bit;
Pardon that fault; once more grant me the place;
And I do swear, even by the same delight,
I will but kiss; I never more will bite.

LXXXIX

Now that of absence the most irksome night
With darkest shade doth overcome my day;
Since Stella's eyes, wont to give me my day,
Leaving my hemisphere, leave me in night;
Each day seems long, and longs for long-stay'd night;
The night, as tedious, woos th' approach of day,
Tired with the dusty toils of busy day,
Languish'd with horrors of the silent night;
Suffering the evils both of day and night,
While no night is more dark than is my day,
Nor no day hath less quiet than my night:
With such bad mixture of my night and day,
That living thus in blackest Winter night,
I feel the flames of hottest Summer day.

XC

Stella, think not that I by verse seek fame,
Who seek, who hope, who love, who live but thee;
Thine eyes my pride, thy lips mine history:
If thou praise not, all other praise is shame.
Nor so ambitious am I, as to frame
A nest for my young praise in laurel tree:
In truth, I swear I wish not there should be
Graved in my epitaph a Poet's name.
Nor, if I would, could I just title make,
That any laud thereof to me should grow,
Without my plumes from others' wings I take:
For nothing from my wit or will doth flow,
Since all my words thy beauty doth indite,
And Love doth hold my hand, and makes me write.

From CERTAIN SONNETS

Leave me, O Love, which reachest but to dust;
And thou, my mind, aspire to higher things;
Grow rich in that which never taketh rust;
Whatever fades, but fading pleasure brings.
Draw in thy beams, and humble all thy might
To that sweet yoke, where lasting freedoms be;
Which breaks the clouds, and opens forth the light
That doth both shine, and give us sight to see.
O take fast hold, let that light be thy guide
In this small course which birth draws out to death,
And think how evil becometh him to slide,
Who seeketh heav'n, and comes of heavenly breath.
Then farewell, world; thy uttermost I see:
Eternal Love, maintain thy Life in me.

Samuel Daniel

From DELIA

IX

If this be love, to draw a weary breath,
Paint on floods, till the shore, cry to th' air;
With downward looks, still reading on the earth
The sad memorials of my love's despair.
If this be love, to war against my soul,
Lie down to wail, rise up to sigh and grieve me,
The never-resting stone of care to roll,
Still to complain my griefs, and none relieve me;
If this be love, to clothe me with dark thoughts,
Haunting untrodden paths to wail apart;
My pleasures horror, music tragic notes,
Tears in my eyes, and sorrow at my heart.
If this be love, to live a living death,
O then love I, and draw this weary breath.

XXXV

Thou canst not die whilst any zeal abound
In feeling hearts, that can conceive these lines;
Though thou, a Laura, hast no Petrach found,
In base attire yet clearly beauty shines.
And I, though born in a colder clime,
Do feel mine inward heat as great (I know it);
He never had more faith, although more rhyme,
I love as well, though he could better show it.
But I may add one feather to thy fame,
To help her flight throughout the fairest isle;
And if my pen could more enlarge thy name,
Then shouldest thou live in an immortal style.
But, though that Laura better limned be,
Suffice, thou shalt be loved as well as she.

XLVI

Let others sing of knights and paladins
In aged accents and untimely words,
Paint shadows in imaginary lines,
Which well the reach of their high wits records.
But I must sing of thee, and those fair eyes
Authentic shall my verse in time to come,
When yet th'unborn shall say, 'Lo where she lies,
Whose beauty made him speak that else was dumb.'
These are the arcs, the trophies I erect,
That fortify thy name against old age,
And these thy sacred virtues must protect
Against the dark, and time's consuming rage.
Though th'error of my youth they shall discover,
Suffice they show I lived and was thy lover.

John Donne

From SONGS AND SONNETS
THE GOOD-MORROW

I wonder, by my troth, what thou and I
Did, till we lov'd? Were we not wean'd till then?
But suck'd on country pleasures, childishly?
Or snorted we in the seven sleepers' den?
'Twas so; but this, all pleasures fancies be.
If ever any beauty I did see,
Which I desir'd, and got, 'twas but a dream of thee.

And now good-morrow to our waking souls,
Which watch not one another out of fear;
For love, all love of other sights controls,
And makes one little room an everywhere.
Let sea-discoverers to new worlds have gone,
Let maps to others, worlds on worlds have shown,
Let us possess one world; each hath one, and is one.

My face in thine eye, thine in mine appears,
And true plain hearts do in the faces rest;
Where can we find two better hemispheres
Without sharp north, without declining west?
What ever dies, was not mixt equally;
If our two loves be one, or, thou and I
Love so alike that none do slacken, none can die.

WOMAN'S CONSTANCY

Now thou hast lov'd me one whole day,
Tomorrow when thou leav'st, what wilt thou say?
Wilt thou then antedate some new made vow?
Or say that now
We are not just those persons, which we were?
Or, that oaths made in reverential fear
Of Love, and his wrath, any may forswear?
Or, as true deaths, true marriages untie,
So lovers' contracts, images of those,
Bind but till sleep, death's image, them unloose?
Or, your own end to justify,
For having purposed change, and falsehood, you
Can have no way but falsehood to be true?
Vain lunatic, against these 'scapes I could
Dispute, and conquer, if I would,
Which I abstain to do,
For by tomorrow, I may think so too.

LOVERS' INFINITENESS

If yet I have not all thy love,
Dear, I shall never have it all,
I cannot breathe one other sigh, to move,
Nor can entreat one other tear to fall.
And all my treasure, which should purchase thee,
Sighs, tears, and oaths, and letters I have spent,
Yet no more can be due to me,
Then at the bargain made was meant.
If then thy gift of love were partial,
That some to me, some should to others fall,
Dear, I shall never have thee all.

Or if then thou gavest me all,
All was but all, which thou hadst then;
But if in thy heart, since, there be or shall
New love created be, by other men,
Which have their stocks entire, and can in tears,
In sighs, in oaths, and letters outbid me,
This new love may beget new fears,
For, this love was not vowed by thee.
And yet it was, thy gift being general,
The ground, thy heart is mine; what ever shall
Grow there, dear, I should have it all.

Yet I would not have all yet,
He that hath all can have no more,
And since my love doth every day admit
New growth, thou shouldst have new rewards in store;
Thou canst not every day give me thy heart,
If thou canst give it, then thou never gav'st it:
Love's riddles are, that though thy heart depart,
It stays at home, and thou with losing sav'st it:
But we will have a way more liberal,
Then changing hearts, to join them, so we shall
Be one, and one another's all.

THE TRIPLE FOOL

I am two fools, I know,
For loving, and for saying so
In whining poetry;
But where's that wise man, that would not be I,
If she would not deny?
Then as th' earth's inward narrow crooked lanes
Do purge sea-water's fretful salt away,
I thought, if I could draw my pains
Through rhyme's vexation, I should them allay.
Grief brought to numbers cannot be so fierce,
For he tames it, that fetters it in verse.

But when I have done so,
Some man, his art and voice to show,
Doth set and sing my pain,
And, by delighting many, frees again
Grief, which verse did restrain.
To love and grief tribute of verse belongs,
But not of such as pleases when 'tis read;
Both are increased by such songs:
For both their triumphs so are published,
And I, which was two fools, do so grow three;
Who are a little wise, the best fools be.

THE TOKEN

Send me some token, that my hope may live,
Or that my easeless thoughts may sleep and rest;
Send me some honey to make sweet my hive,
That in my passion I may hope the best.
I beg no riband wrought with thine own hands,
To knit our loves in the fantastic strain
Of new-touched youth; nor ring to show the stands
Of our affection, that as that's round and plain,
So should our loves meet in simplicity;
No, nor the corals which thy wrist enfold,
Laced up together in congruity,
To show our thoughts should rest in the same hold;
No, nor thy picture, though most gracious,
And most desired, because best like the best;
Nor witty lines, which are most copious,
Within the writings which thou hast addressed.

Send me nor this, nor that, to increase my store,
But swear thou thinkst I love thee, and no more.

THE MESSAGE

Send home my long strayed eyes to me,
Which (oh) too long have dwelt on thee,
Yet since there they have learned such ill,
Such forced fashions,
And false passions,
That they be
Made by thee
Fit for no good fight, keep them still.

Send home my harmless heart again,
Which no unworthy thought could stain,
But if it be taught by thine
To make jestings
Of protestings,
And cross both
Word and oath,
Keep it, for then 'tis none of mine.

Yet fend me back my heart and eyes,
That I may know, and see thy lies,
And may laugh and joy, when though
Art in anguish
And dost languish
For some one
That will none,
Or prove as false as thou art now.

John Milton

I

O Nightingale, that on yon bloomy spray
Warblest at ever, when all the woods are still,
Thou with fresh hope the lover's heart dost fill,
While the jolly hours lead on propitious May,
Thy liquid notes that close the eye of day,
First heard before the shallow cuckoo's bill
Portend success in love; O if Jove's will
Have linked that amorous power to thy soft lay,
Now timely sing, ere the rude bird of hate
Foretell my hopeless doom in some grove nigh:
As thou from year to year hast sung too late
For my relief; yet hadst no reason why,
Whether the muse, or Love call thee his mate,
Both them I serve, and of their train am I.

IX

Lady, that in the prime of earliest youth,
Wisely hast shunned the broad way and the green,
And with those few are eminently seen,
That labour up the hill of heavenly truth,
The better part with Mary and with Ruth,
Chosen thou hast, and they that overween,
And at thy growing virtues fret their spleen,
No anger find in thee, but pity and ruth.
Thy care is fixed, and zealously attends
To fill thy odorous lamp with deeds of light,
And hope that reaps not shame. Therefore be sure
Thou, when the bridegroom with his feastful friends
Passes to bliss at the mid-hour of night,
Hast gained thy entrance, virgin wise and pure.

Index of First Lines

Notes on Illustrations